# Unseen Feelings

## *Untold Thoughts*

-S. Mubashshira Fatma

*For You,*
*To explore*
*inside of You...*

Because You are Perfect as you are.

# Index

# Index

## *You & You Only*

You have given up on you now,
and trying to change your
choice now.
One step, but you back down.
Why? Because you think people
are much cool, making you feel
like a fool.

But you don't know, what's here
just in you.

Be a human of you and you only,
you're the one and one only.
Not tryna what you're not,

Not the one you just caught.
It will take a cost and will make
you forget who really you are,
who really you are.

Follow then forget,
some parts of yourself,
just don't change what you have,
What you are.

Jealous tryna change you, better
tryna face you.
The cover of your story, Can just
blame you. But don't move it
and try to choose it.

Choosing will be the best then
let forget.
You know, be a human of you
and you only, you're the one and
one only.

## *All in your head*

'I never know, who am I?
Don't know if I am enough for
me.
Where am I trying to reach?
Get me thinking like I am
nothing.'

You can do what you wanna do,
You can be the one you wanna
be.

Keep in your mind, it's all in
your head,
You never try to motivate
yourself.

Don't think you are less,
Don't think you are a mess.
You could be the one that you
are becoming to be.
You could feel the vibe of going
out of your league.

Just never let people get in your
head.
If you are thinking" what will
they think of? What if I fail?"
Then ask "Will you not get what
you are capable of?
Why Are You Here For Then?
Why Are You Here For Then?”

## *Why am I Not Enough?*

They know what to expect,
they are thinking I could be like
them,
But I'm just a human being,
Who doesn't know how to
express a thing.
Trying my best to forget all
embarrassment,
starting a new scene but never
know when?
Trying my best to make my
dreams come alive,
They have their own dreams,
I can't take their flight.

Why do they think I'm not
enough?
Why do they want that I'm not?
I just wanna be who I'm not
enough for you, but for me.

Starting to understand that
might coming from within,
growing automatically.
Don't want you to tell me it's
time to grow up.
I can understand, just by seeing
stuff.
Is that not growing up?

Why do they think I'm not
enough?
Why do they want that I'm not?
I just wanna who I'm not
enough for you, but for me.

Why do, day by day, they think
it's time to change?
I know who I am, and I don't
want to change.
Just don't wanna ask me who
you are. Who are you in there?
But you're not me.

## *Another Energy*

Feels like I'm here all alone,
Feels like I have to do it on my
own,
I know you are trying to help
me,
But for me, you're breaking my
dreams.

There is not only one thing, it's
life,
If one story closes, one opens,
It will keep continuing till my
last.

I think you keep forbidding it, but it's just not my dream, it's my heart.

Hey, Can't you say it, you are just hurting my pride, by talking round and round but it's one thing.

I know that I can't take it, whether you say it or not.

It's like another energy.

I keep hating it when you act like supporting.

For the first time ever, I thought
that I had quit my dreams a lot.
But it's not like those once,
it's connected to my heart
because whenever I think it's
not going to work,I feel like
crying.

That's it, it's not like the
previous one.
It's not them anymore, it's for
myself.
It's like another energy, it's
unique.

I never thought I could get so
attached to a dream,
it's like another energy.

## *That Will, That Feel*

If you take it, you can make it,
If you dream it, you can't
hesitate it.
That's the truth, you can't move.
You know what? It's up to you.

You know what you can do, so
no matter what you can't lose.
It can take once or twice or
maybe too much to cause, it is
time to forget your flaws.

You couldn't lose if you have
that will, if you have that feel.

It's a feeling you can't reject, that's a meaning that you got a reason to cross your limits.

If you have that will, if you have that feel.

## *Proud of Myself*

I don't know why am I like this?
(Not proud of me)
Kind of think I can make it,
But it's just one side thinking.
Full of false me, what's within
me is not me.
Not the one I thought I was to
be. (so false)

I keep regretting it so I need to
forget it so that I don't lose
myself.

Please be me, real me.
Let me see, real me.

I want to be proud of myself,
But I didn't made it too well.

Those things I messed up so
bad,
Now I'm the reason for me to be
sad.
Lose all those things I respect,
finally I'm back to my sense.

## *Those Precious Things*

What am I trying to be?
Where am I trying to reach?
Fulfil the needs that I need.
Is it that only you feel?

I want to be that one who can
live their dreams,
who has no limits more than
they reach the peak.
I think I know what all think,
I think I can understand that
feeling.
But it's just one thing keep
going on,

they have their dreams that they
think if they did.
They would leave those Precious
Things behind that they don't
wanna leave.

I felt that I meant that all,
But now that I am here, it's all,
really hard for me,

To leave those precious things...

## *Wanna Travel*

The more I live, The more I feel,
The feeling of travelling to
reach.
Somewhere I will go,
Somewhere to reach,
I can't let it go so let it be.

By living through the dreams I
built,
By surviving to end till I do,
By controlling the fate I get.
I am making own fate to get
through,
By not letting my dreams loose.

## *I am F*

‘Hey, I failed,
Is it really over if I care?’
After everything you been
through,
You still couldn't get through.

It's Okay if you're feeling like a
loser,
But you know you only got more
closer.

You have just started to take
your goal seriously,

And now you have to play your
game professionally you ain't
lost yet,
You got your first loss in a
match and it ain't over yet.

You've got to make it your
strength,
And show everyone you can go
to what length.

That is What called a
"comeback of a Hero".

So it's your choice if it's F for
failure or F for forging ahead.

## *Memories Stay,People Don't*

Standing here, All alone,
Still a smile that wouldn't go.
Losing me, lost my control,
Still bright eyes that wouldn't
low.

Because it's not the feeling of a
loneliness,
It's a heart full of love and care,
With the memories, we can't let
it go,
That makes us feel, we wouldn't
be alone.

Memories stay, People don't.
Not letting you go would be
cold.
You would be vanish in front of
my sight,
But it's good to feel you were on
my side.

Unknown smile, starting to
mount,
Almost a tear dropping down.
In front it's not the same,
It's the memories that's back
again.

They will be my proof of you,

That we were something true.
You were something to me and I
was something to you.

Memories stay, People don't,
Not letting you go would be
cold.
You would be vanish in front of
my sight,
But it's good to feel you were on
my side.

'You are still here'

## *Silent story*

I have found myself still empty,
Don't know why I am half of me.
I want to say something.
Want to Express I want to tell
them, But why does my voice
not reach them? Where it has to
be?

Why is my voice a silent story?
Want to talk to them, it's half of
my dream.

I told a word to start,
But it disappeared somewhere
too far,

Didn't know it was even there.
Calm me down to fight me out,
But can't it be easy, like it's for
them,
I covered it out, I covered
myself.

## *Miss You*

I have to say it, it is so hard,
To be in the present but still
want the past.
I can't forget, all memories we
have together,
But now, I really want it all to
gather.
Even if I don't show you, it's not
the truth.

I wish we still be like we were
then,
Never wanted this story to end.
Even if we have to last, I really
want to start again.

I don't know if you know, but it
was the time that always made
me feel like myself.

Now, I really see you in
daydreams,
I really miss you from my heart.
I want us to be like when we
were small,
I never want to grow if it means,
We have to grow apart.

I don't know if you really know,
but I don't want to let you go.

## *My Real Life*

I have longed many times,
To go and see that world.
I have longed many times,
To meet and have that fun.

Sometimes I wanna go out with
them and see,
But sometimes I felt like staying
in my small space with me.
It's so hard to leave that comfort
zone for me.

I wanna feel free and live real
life,

Find my story and call that
mine.

Go on trips, have friends, spend
times with everyone I meet,
Don't think much, have my
family and friends
around making my mind free.
We are all together, laughing,
playing and they teasing me.

It is all I wanna crave of my
living times,
It is all I wanna crave of my life
that I can call mine.

I wanna feel free and live real
life,
Find my story and call that
mine.

## *Can't Believe It*

The things we did, it's a past.
I have to say, it was too fast.
We have it all in our fate, at
least in our way.
It never or ever will fade away.
I can't forget it, even if it wanna
go away.

I can't believe it, it will be too
fast,
I can't believe it, it is to last,
I can't believe it, we made it
cast,
Now it is the start of a new start.

Can't really think what will we
get,
But things will change ahead.
We are growing now as to
growing apart,
I can't imagine it.
How will I fit in?
How will I know where I
belong?

Everything will fade away in the
ashes of memories.

## *Let Me Try*

From the start, The first to love
me.
Never made me feel lonely.
The first to ever be , for me.
From the start, the first to ever
live.
Always there for me.
The first to make me feel happy.

The way you care silently,
Push me high to make me fly.
The way you cry silently,
So that, I don't have to worry.
So now, take my shoulder to cry,
At Least let me try.

I never wanted to let you down,
Now I am at the ground.
Let me try, let me be your
shoulder to cry.

Now let me care for you, like
you did for me.
Let me be there for you, like you
are there for me.
Let me fill your pain with all the
memories we have gained.
Let me always be there for you...

## *Feeling Lame*

I have caught me thinking
again, That,
Why am I feeling lame.
Everybody is doing something
with their lives,
And here I am feeling ashamed.

I am stuck in this part of my
time,
And they are moving towards
their aims.
Why is it that they are happy?
And here I am feeling lame.

Those old times are coming to
me,
Where I used to feel the line
between.
Where I am sitting alone at the
last desk,
And they are all over nowhere
near to face.
That can be my trauma of my
old school,
No friends, No call, everyday's
the same to look.

Now that I am out of it,
Still not near to them,
Why do I feel that way again?

## *Outta The Dark*

Long last, finally, I'm outta the dark,
I have my insecurities, but it's still part of my job.
Longing to show everyone what I've got,
It's too late, but it got to take a lot.

It will take a lot, sure.

I've expected everything that I wouldn't accept,

It’s a journey even if I fail it’s
there to show what I shouldn’t
do again,
I'll Learn a lesson from there.

I am outta the dark, even if it’s
just for short.
Like I’m still finding, What’s
here for me?
What should I cherish?
What’s there for me?
What can I hold?
What’s there not for me to be? If
it’s for me?
But I’m sure, It’s somewhere out
there for me.

## Hear Me !

Many stuff going on my mind,
It's something measly so please
don't mind.
I guess it's easy to say I'm fine,
So "I'm fine, I'm fine".

Last time I looked it up,
Showing how easy going is my
life.
They say you're lucky, you are
fine.

But if only one time I say that
I want some answers to go with
my life,

I say I can't handle my thoughts
and time,
If I say I ain't alright
Would you hear me out?
Would you help me out?

If I say that I'm fine then cure
me out,
If I say get out of my sight then
say you wanna hear me out.
Because I need someone to hold
on to let it all out.

So force me to talk and hear me
out.

## *Irregular Phase*

It's fine, The words I say now
don't mind,
It's an anger of a kind,
It wouldn't even matter after
some time.
It's the words I mould until now,
It's the flood I hold up to now.

I've reached that limit where I
can say it's the line.
I've got to that stage where you
wouldn't know who came?
where you would say who are
you mate?

I would blabber out words that I
never mean.
I would show the face that I'm
keen to lean.

A sudden blow, even I don't
know, why did I do so?
So if I get to that stage please
forgive me, mate.

## *Infinite Tears*

My head hurts, My heart aches.
There are no words, Only left
with Infinite tears.
I can't find any helping hand,
Only me, Inside an lonely room,
Crying , Just crying it all out.
There is no going back, all that
is painful regret.

All the pains that you were
holding back.
Don't hold back now.
You will have to stay strong
again,

You will have to find your way
in this world.
You will have to find your place.
No words, just fight your
infinite tears.

## Words For You

## Words For You

# Words For You

# Words For You

Printed by Libri Plureos GmbH in Hamburg,
Germany